Visitor/Guest Log

By Joshua R. Embry

Date:	Visitor Name:	Meeting with:	Purpose:

Date:	Visitor Name:	Meeting with:	Purpose:

Date:	Visitor Name:	Meeting with:	Purpose:

Date:	Visitor Name:	Meeting with:	Purpose:

Date:	Visitor Name:	Meeting with:	Purpose:

Date:	Visitor Name:	Meeting with:	Purpose:

Date:	Visitor Name:	Meeting with:	Purpose:

Date:	Visitor Name:	Meeting with:	Purpose:

Date:	Visitor Name:	Meeting with:	Purpose:

Date:	Visitor Name:	Meeting with:	Purpose:

Date:	Visitor Name:	Meeting with:	Purpose:

Date:	Visitor Name:	Meeting with:	Purpose:

Date:	Visitor Name:	Meeting with:	Purpose:

Date:	Visitor Name:	Meeting with:	Purpose:

Date:	Visitor Name:	Meeting with:	Purpose:

Date:	Visitor Name:	Meeting with:	Purpose:

Date:	Visitor Name:	Meeting with:	Purpose:

Date:	Visitor Name:	Meeting with:	Purpose:

Date:	Visitor Name:	Meeting with:	Purpose:

Date:	Visitor Name:	Meeting with:	Purpose:

Date:	Visitor Name:	Meeting with:	Purpose:

Date:	Visitor Name:	Meeting with:	Purpose:

Date:	Visitor Name:	Meeting with:	Purpose:

Date:	Visitor Name:	Meeting with:	Purpose:

Date:	Visitor Name:	Meeting with:	Purpose:

Date:	Visitor Name:	Meeting with:	Purpose:

Date:	Visitor Name:	Meeting with:	Purpose:

Date:	Visitor Name:	Meeting with:	Purpose:

Date:	Visitor Name:	Meeting with:	Purpose:

Date:	Visitor Name:	Meeting with:	Purpose:

Date:	Visitor Name:	Meeting with:	Purpose:

www.ingramcontent.com/pod-product-compliance
Lightning Source LLC
Chambersburg PA
CBHW081315180526
45170CB00007B/2720